THE ANTHOLOGY OF THE RIO GRANDE VALLEY INTERNATIONAL POETRY FESTIVAL

BOUNDLESS
2024

FLOWERSONG
PRESS

SELECTED & EDITED BY

ÉRIKA ELISA GARZA TAMEZ
AND EDWARD VIDAURRE

FLOWERSONG
PRESS

FlowerSong Press
McAllen, Texas 78501
Copyright © 2024 FlowerSong Press

ISBN: 978-1-963245-58-5

Published by FlowerSong Press
in the United States of America.
www.flowersongpress.com

Set in Adobe Garamond Pro

Edited by Érika Elisa Garza Tamez and Edward Vidaurre
Cover Design by Priscilla Celina Suarez

NOTICE: SCHOOLS AND BUSINESSES
FlowerSong Press offers copies of this book at quantity discount with bulk
purchase for educational, business, or sales promotional use. For information,
please email the Publisher at info@flowersongpress.com.

Table of Contents

V.I.P.F.

RIO GRANDE VALLEY INTERNATIONAL POETRY FESTIVAL

Boundless is the official anthology of the Rio Grande Valley International Poetry Festival (VIPF), founded in 2008 by Daniel García Ordaz and Brenda Nettles Riojas. VIPF is held annually the last weekend in April in deep South Texas as a celebration of National Poetry Month. Directed by Edward Vidaurre.

WWW.VALLEYPOETRYFEST.ORG

Dedication

IN HONOR OF:

Jan Seale. 2012 Texas State Poet Laureate, McAllen, Texas
Emmy Pérez, 2020 Texas Poet Laureate, McAllen, Texas
Daniel García Ordaz, 2023 City of McAllen Poet Laureate

IN MEMORIAM:

Dr. Gloria Evangelina Anzaldúa
Jovita González
Dr. Américo Paredes
Raúl R. Salinas
Trinidad Sánchez

BOUNDLESS

2024

THE ANTHOLOGY OF THE
RIO GRANDE VALLEY
INTERNATIONAL POETRY FESTIVAL

WHAT'S IN A NAME?
ON MISLABELING "VIOLENCE"

by Sara Bawany

In 1983, a baby orca now known as Tilikum was captured off the coast of Iceland and sold to an aquarium for entertainment. In the wild, orcas swim anywhere between 40 to 140 miles per day but he was held captive in a 31' x 23' x 12' tank when he wasn't performing, along with two older female orcas. Their training consisted of punishments like collective food deprivation if even one of them made a mistake. As a result, the other orcas lashed out and abused Tilikum for years, leaving bloody teeth marks across his body each morning.

-

Decades ago, a group of displaced and traumatized people made their way to a promised land. Centuries ago, another group of explorers seeking glory and adventure arrived at the shore of a land mass they didn't know existed. Both groups — hundreds of years apart — were welcomed warmly, peacefully, by its natives despite their varied cultures, languages, and skin color.

Before long, through secret treaties and written declarations unbeknownst to the natives, both groups of newcomers demanded the land for themselves. Celebrations and gatherings turned violent as the visitors demolished native villages, slaughtered their food sources, and forced them from their homes, while claiming them as their own. *God has willed it!* they declared. By their Manifest Destiny, the natives' destiny became manifest.

The natives retaliated, fighting for their home, their land, their trees, their freedom. The colonizers, outraged at their fury, called them *barbaric, savage, inhuman, animals, violent* — and then massacred the majority of them, succeeding in removing the rest from their own land. One side demanded freedom while the other side demanded for their deaths, while simultaneously claiming victimhood. This is how you systematically dehumanize an entire people.

Today, the descendants of those natives live on small strips of land the once-guests designated to them, their resources cut off, and imprisoned within a place where, for generations, they had lived freely. Sanitized, uniform buildings erected by the new empire sit staunchly on top of what was once farmland, homes, and even graves. Within the small strips of land, food deserts exist in abundance. Children are malnourished. The people are regulated, deprecated, and decimated through disease. But this imprisonment has never been deemed as violence.

Violence's shape goes beyond bullets and bloodshed. Violence is a cage. Violence is not being allowed to leave a place you've been forced to call home. Violence is being cornered so tightly you can not breathe.

Experts say that those exposed to violence from a young age suffer from post-traumatic stress and even psychosis — this applies to humans, orcas, or other creatures. However, there is no diagnosis in the DSM for experiencing violence on a regular basis which follows into adulthood and old age. People living in these "reservations," "territories," have something so beyond Post Traumatic Stress Disorder, there isn't even a name for it in our language.

-

Around the age of 8, I watched all the *Free Willy* movies for the first time on the small, boxy TV in our living room. I was drawn to the story of the young boy who rebelled against the animal entertainment industry and successfully released the orca, Willy, from a theme park's small tank. I was fascinated by Willy, and by creatures like him, how it was possible for something so enormous to be forced into confinement and still remain so gentle and so intelligent.

I was a budding young artist and author by this time, and I put together my own version of an encyclopedia — on notebook paper and drawn with a no.

2 pencil — about whales, including its own glossary, index, and elaborate illustrations. In the scraps of paper I deemed a book, there is what I will generously call a surrealist drawing of a little boy with his arms wrapped all the way around an orca in an embrace, something quite impossible given an orca's size. But it perhaps encompassed a naive idealism I held at that age that if we reached out our arms and stretched our humanity far enough, we could save and shelter everyone that came under our care.

I chuckle every time I flip the delicate pages, almost 20 years old by now. The first page of chapter 5 has *Save the Whales* in big block letters. Throughout the book, the writing occasionally and abruptly switches to cursive font while my childhood self staunchly addresses orcas harming humans as an anomaly: *This does NOT mean whales are bad.*

-

In 1991, Tilikum drowned one of his trainers, and public attention forced the aquarium's closure. He was transferred to another tank, and housed with more hostile orcas, he continued to suffer.

It's not really known what turns a nonviolent creature into a murderer except the violence done to them. There is no data of orcas viciously killing in the wild. But put them in a cage, let them wake up bloody each morning, and you have given them a new name. Violence does indeed beget violence, but we are so good at erasing history, aren't we? We are so good at pretending the truth isn't staring at us behind glass or bars, so good at naming something violence when it is actually a direct response to pain.

And what's in a name? The name *Tilikum* in Chinook jargon means *friend, common people, relationship, tribe*, yet the term *killer whale* persists. Orca becomes killer whale. People shoved into cages or bombed to smithereens become *terrorists, violent, barbaric* when they finally fight back. *Colonizer* becomes *victim, oppressor* becomes *oppressed*.

-

In the story of Adam's creation, the angels, recognizing humanity's capability for great destruction, questioned God for the first time in their existence.

Do the angels know us better than we know ourselves?

The hunger for power drives humans to put others in cages again and again, and we are appalled when the captives bite back. *Aggressor, oppressor, terrorist, monster* — we who pride ourselves on our values of freedom, put a stamp of disapproval on others for demanding their own.

When Black Lives Matter protests erupted in the summer of 2020, some smashed windows led to several treading backwards. *Condemn the violence! Stop the violence!* the other side shouted. And we succumbed, flailed.

After 9/11, every time a suicide bomber blows himself up, Muslims collectively get on social media and feel the need to apologize, to condemn the act, to remind white Americans over and over that we do not support the violence. But why are those who cultivated these seeds of violence given a pass?

-

On October 7th, 2023, several natives of occupied Palestine broke through the walls of cages that imprisoned them and their people for no crime except their ethnicities. In retaliation, white phosphorus clouds rained down thousands of bombs, brutally murdering Palestinian civilians and burying countless more under rubble.

On October 11th, 2023, four days later, our president claimed to have seen 40 beheaded Israeli babies with his own eyes. His own staff retracted his statement as false, with no apology issued. But thousands of children in Gaza had already paid the price. Lies are the best fuel for violence and our government fanned its flames.

Similarly, a million Iraqis were killed in the early 2000s because someone lied about "weapons of mass destruction." There is yet to be an apology for that "mistake."

-

In 2010, Tilikum killed another one of his trainers. The aquarium hid his history from the public until investigative reporters uncovered the trail of deaths. The slow outrage began, but Tilikum was nearly 30 years old by then and dying.

Tilikum killed three people because those who held him captive followed the money instead of acknowledging that he was going insane from the abuse and confinement. He sired twenty-one offspring in captivity, and was known as the aquarium's *chief sperm bank*. It's quite marvelous what we produce when we control each other. Occupation is good for control. Control is good for pocketbooks. Fat pocketbooks are good for power, and the cycle continues.

On October 14th, 2023, three days after the president's false statement, defense stocks were at an all-time high. 8 billion dollars were casually dropped into Israel's bloody hands earlier in the week while millions of Americans continued to beg for a reprieve from student loan debt, from the widespread housing crisis. Violence and war are good for the economy, they say, although the majority never see that payoff. But *Stop the violence!* is only bellowed when violence stops being beneficial for those inciting it in the first place.

-

Humans back each other and other creatures into corners and demand submission until the captives fight back. Headlines then read, *Unprecedented violence breaks out!* or *Historians explore possible causes for backlash.*

There is something particularly insidious and arrogant about our tax dollars working diligently to erase entire cities from maps, and then our leaders attempting to erase history, renaming entire narratives to suit them better. There is something even more insidious in our belief that we can control things bigger than us. Orcas. Entire nations.

Hope.

Excerpt: Violence does indeed beget violence, but we are so good at erasing history, aren't we? We are so good at pretending the truth isn't staring at us behind glass or bars, so good at naming something violence when it is actually a direct response to pain.

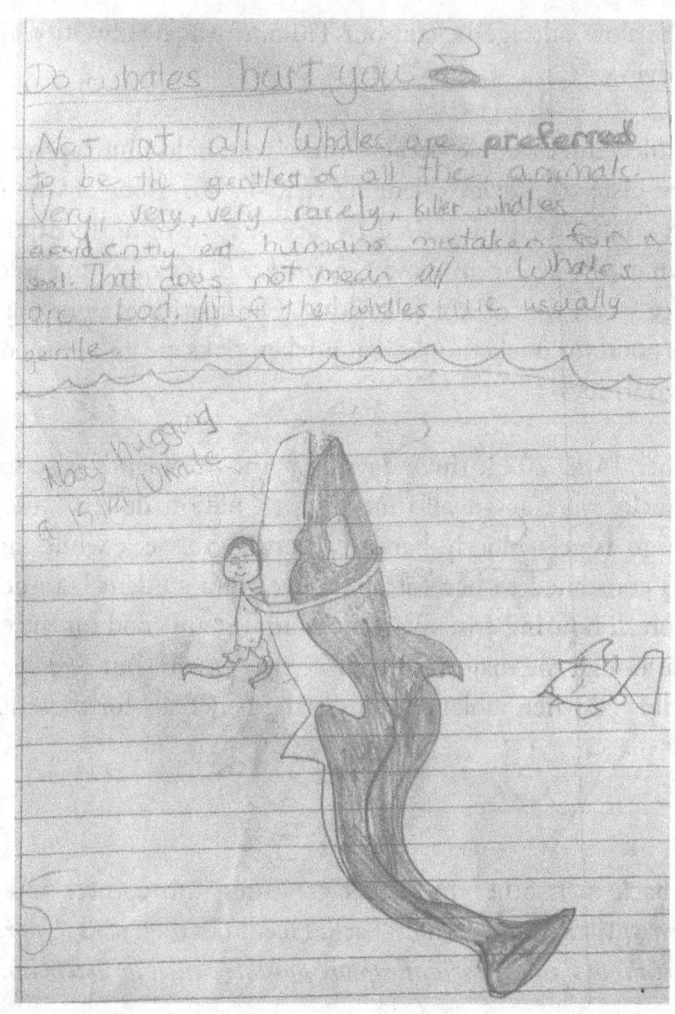

Photo description: A drawing from 8-year-old Sara's "book" on whales

This essay was first published in infrarrealistas.org.

Bio: Sara Bawany is a clinical social worker and second-year MFA Poetry student at Texas State University. She published *(w)holehearted: a collection of poetry and prose* in 2018, and her second book, *Quarter Life Crisis*, was published in October 2023. She is the Assistant Managing Editor at Porter House Review and serves as a mentor and instructor at House of Amal, a writing institution for Muslim youth. You can find more about her at www.sarabawany.com.

ABRIR LOS OJOS AL FUTURO

por Alejandro Zapata Espinosa

Abrir los ojos al futuro
hidratarlos con agua lluvia
sostenerlos con ganchos

No permitir que la resequedad
las venas coaguladas
el lagrimal saturado
parpadeen
el irrepetible
crecimiento de levadura
de la bomba atómica

Reseña: Alejandro Zapata Espinosa (Colombia, 2002): estudiante de Licenciatura en Literatura y Lengua Castellana. Ocupó el segundo puesto en el XVIII Concurso de Cuento Tomás Carrasquilla del Tecnológico de Antioquia (2021). Mención de Honor en el 79º Concurso Internacional de Poesía y Narrativa Camino de Palabras (2023).

ANOTHER MILITARY COUP

by Michael Shoemaker

shallow breathing - high piercing sirens screech in the streets -
crouching shoulders - whispers -
fences keeping enemies of the state in - keeping the will of the people out -
curfew enforced - four checkpoints to cross the city -
barricades - identification and documents key everywhere -
demonstrations of force by authorities to threaten underground resistance -
- an injury here - a disappearance there -
no assembly of groups over six people - the pounding of a door -
entrance without warrant - yanking of an old man from his bed of slumber
- furrowed brows -

food lines - scarcity -
mother covering the mouth of her crying baby to not call attention -
puppet polling stations - secret police -
false accusations of neighbors for safety - betrayal -
the stench of burning books and uncollected trash -
no electricity - all Internet down - suspicion - one shot -
entering a fleeing young man's arching back - he crumples on the sidewalk in
a pool of his own blood -
a warning to all of us - the spirit and fight for liberty continues.

Global freedom declined for the 17th consecutive year.
New coups and other attempts to undermine representative government
destabilized Burkina Faso, Tunisia, Peru, and Brazil. Previous years' coups
and ongoing repression continued to diminish basic liberties in Guinea
and constrain those in Turkey, Myanmar, and Thailand, among others.
—Freedom House, September, 2023, https://freedomhouse.org/report/
freedom-world/2023/marking-50-years

Bio: Michael Shoemaker is a poet, writer, and photographer. His writing has appeared in *Last Leaves Literary Magazine*, *Front Porch Review*, and in anthologies at *Poetry Pacific* and *Pure Slush*. He lives in Magna, Utah. He is the author of "Rocky Mountain Reflections" which can be purchased at https://poetschoice.in/beta/product/rocky-mountain-reflections/.

THE HARKENING CROW: LINGUISTIC SEMIOSIS IN 4 DILATIONS

by Tezozomoc

Semiosis: "...borders are the semiosphere's most important structural and functional positions. Borders constitute temporary (psychological) ontologies, and sociopolitical ontologies. In other words, the semiotic structural mechanisms for worlding(s), underlying the political practices of territorialization and community-formation behind already (seemingly) stabilized worlds. Borders establish social relations and structure the field in which it is possible to recognize someone (no matter the species) as a social actor or being in the first place."
　　　　　　　　—*Ott Puumeister, et. al.,*
　　　　　　　　　　"Semiosis is always at the border, which operates it."

In yonder post, there perched a crow so proud,
Enjoying dewy morning's gentle shroud.
Pondering where to find his next repast,
Amidst the farmland and pistachios vast.

He sits and harkens to the darkling day,
Surveying the workers in their array.
The helicopters spray the grass with care,
To feed the cows, who graze without a care.

The crow clucks away, a sound so sweet,
As sun's reflection off the copters' fleet,
Catches his eyes and draws him in so deep,
Into the darkness where his secrets keep.

Oh crow, thou art a creature of the air,
Soaring high on wings without a care.

May thy flight be free and thy heart be light,
As thou searches for thy sustenance with might.

Hay un crow aterrizando en mi fence post
Posado, disfrutando el morning dew
Reflexionando sobre la búsqueda de comida en farmland
Cubierto de pistachio trees comenzando a blossom

Se sienta allí, escuchando la oscuridad del día
Meditando sobre el camino a seguir en su flight
Planeando su próxima tarea en el cielo
El crow sigue su camino, siempre en sight

Un crow landed on my fence post without fear
Perched and enjoying the morning dew so clear
Pondering the search for food on farmland so green
Covered by pistachio trees just starting to glean

He sits there harkening the darkness of the day
Surveying the Mexican farm workers in dismay
Pesticide helicopters spray the checks of Sudan grass
For the cows that will soon come and be fed.

The crow clucks away as the glitter from the sun
Reflects off the helicopter and catches his attention
Taken in by his darkness, he continues to watch
As the helicopter eventually flies out of his march.

En mi fence post, hay un crow landing
Disfrutando el morning dew, perched en su lugar
Reflexionando sobre la búsqueda de alimento
En farmland cubierto por pistachio trees en bloom

Harkening la darkness del día, se sienta allí
Observando a los mexicanos en su trabajo diario
Los helicópteros de pesticidas rocían las praderas de Sudan grass
Para las vacas, y el crow hace clic en el aire

El resplandor del sol en los helicópteros
Atrae su mirada, y su oscuridad lo absorbe
El crow sigue observando, sin decir nada
Elevando su vuelo, en busca de su destino y su verdad.

Yo, check it, there's a crow on my fence post,
Perched up high, enjoying the morning's most,
Pondering where to find his next meal,
Farmland covered in pistachios, a tasty deal.

He sits there, harkening to the darkness of the day,
Surveying Mexican workers, hard at work without delay,
Helicopters spraying pesticides in the air,
Keeping cows fed, without a single care.

The crow clucks away, taking in the sights,
Glitter from the sun, reflecting really bright,
Off the helicopters, shining in the sky,
Taken in by the darkness, the crow can't deny.

This bird flies high, bien marihuano through the air,
Searching for comezon, without a single care,
May his flight be gratis, and his heart be light,
As the crow continues on his endless flight.

Bio: Tezozomoc is a Los Angeles Chicano Essayist, Poet and 2009 Oscar Nominated Activist, internationally published and has been published by Amoxcalco Books for "I am not your Chihuahua", and by Floricanto Press, "Gashes!: Poems and Pain from the halls of injustice", a collection of poetry, ISBN-13: 978-1951088040, 9/2019. Featured nationally and internationally across zoom open virtual mics. Published in the following journals/anthologies: *2021 Boundless Anthology*, 1/20/2022, *MacroMicroCosm, Healing Hands*, Vol 7 Issue #3, BC, Canada, 4/15/2021, *Rigorous Journal*, 9/21/2020, *Red Earth Productions & Cultural Work*, 12/17/2019, *Underwood Press*, 9/9/2019, *Mom Egg Review, Los Angeles Poets for Justice*, 03/15/2021.

ATACAMA

by Roxane Llanque

My blood flows back
to the oldest desert in the world.
My heart sings softly in Aymara
- where the past lies before you -
this ever-fading cloud bank tune.

The past of me
is trapped in the rain shadow of the Andes.

There, that dancing breeze
Fata Morgana or Cholita bailando?
Skirts layered like scorching air
Black braids on aguayo like flowers -
I never dared to wear the bombín.

The past of me
is trapped in the rain shadow of the Andes.

My Pachamama spark
is a dormant seed of the misty desert.
One day, the clouding questions
and seething Altiplano eyes
will brew a mist so powerful -

The past of me overcomes
the rain shadow of the Andes.
And I shall return as rainfall
to Atacama's desert bloom.

Bio: Roxane Llanque is a Bolivian-German writer and filmmaker. She is the director of the award-winning short film "Aberration" and her story "The Tell-Tale Present" won the 2023 Outstanding Miniature of World Pride Australia. Her writing was published in *Libertine* and *Flint Magazine* and is forthcoming in the anthology *Backyard Earth*.

I CAN ONLY BE ME

by Linda M. Crate

you wouldn't ask a river
to be a mountain,
so why do you ask me to
be anyone but me?

the mythology of my bones
is worth knowing,
the songs and lyrics of my
soul beautiful as they
are scarred;
the garden of my heart
can only open to those whom i trust—

i am not perfect,
but i am a moon with
a rainbow heart and pure intentions;

i want us all to make it,
but i cannot trust
someone
who asks me to be any light
other than mine.

Bio: Linda M. Crate (she/her) is a Pennsylvanian writer whose poetry, short stories, articles, and reviews have been published in a myriad of magazines both online and in print. She has twelve published chapbooks, the latest being: *Searching Stained Glass Windows For An Answer* (Alien Buddha Publishing, December 2022). Her debut book of photography *Songs of the Creek* (Alien Buddha Publishing, April 2023) was recently published.

CREENCIAS

por Ariel Tomás Izquierdo

Al nombrar las cosas que me rodean,
siluetas de lo que creía ya no estar
aparecen
como una poda rara,
objetos mágicos:
una cajita de cassette amarilla
haciendo de caracola,
los sonidos de una
acuarela
brasileña;

un gato azul a rayas con la cola erecta hace infinitos
entre mis pies:
cariño, cariño. También lo creía
de una raza
extinta.

Reseña: Ariel Tomás Izquierdo (Buenos Aires, Argentina, 1984). Asistió a talleres de poesía coordinados por los poetas Osvaldo Bossi, Walter Cassara y César Bandin Ron. Poemas suyos forman parte de antologías, revistas y blogs. https://www.instagram.com/galgo.zen/

PROPHECY IN SILVER

by Joseph A Farina

the first frost
visible only on rooftops
this early october's morning
conveys
its silent silvery spell
on all of us

hearts
beat in rhythm
with the slowing earth
blood
coursing to lunar winds
warms crimson
as apples
ready to harvest
seeds sleeping
dream their
resurrection
fixed in frozen wombs

in polar hemispheres
we gather
adorn with sprigs of evergreen
tables heavy with tubers and gourds
together in ancient prayers
light the first fires
warding away
the pending
winter's oblivion

Bio: Joseph A Farina is a retired lawyer and award winning poet, in Sarnia, Ontario, Canada. His poems have appeared in *Philadelphia Poets, Tower Poetry, The Windsor Review,* and *Tamaracks: Canadian Poetry for the 21st Century.* He has two books of poetry published, *The Cancer Chronicles* and *The Ghosts of Water Street.*

THE MEADOW GIRL

by SP Singh

The eyes betray the feelings
>Though heart beholds,
At every meeting that becomes
>Short as time unfolds,

Kind messages that pass daily
>Through gestures,
In which touch of the hand opens
>Heart apertures,

It captures a beautiful image on
>The walls,
Full of splendor, bliss, innocence
>As night falls,

Sentiments that lay hidden, one
>Passionate look unleashes,
Every activity, every work, your
>Arrival freezes,

Kind letters that write a heart's
>Deep history,
One touch of fondness and the
>Rest is mystery.

Bio: SP Singh, an army veteran, is a novelist, short story writer and painter. His debut novel, 'Parrot under the Pine Tree' was shortlisted for the Best Fiction Award at the Gurgaon Literary Festival and nominated at the Valley of Words Literary Festival in 2018. His short story, 'Palak Dil,' won the South Asian Award for Micro Fiction in 2019. His story, 'The Broken Window' was published in UNSAID, An Asian Anthology by Penguin Random House SEA in 2022 and 'Cherrapunji' has been published in an anthology, 'No One Should Kiss a Frog'. His work has appeared in international magazines and anthologies, including the military anthologies in India.

PAINTER

by John Chinaka Onyeche

The world a void vast and unadorned,
A canvas unfamiliar to brown skin's glare,
Another arrived his world to paint anew,
Brushstrokes of cruelty brutality's sort.

He sat upon ship's deck silent and meek,
A sheep shipped voiceless lost and frail,
Their books' words seeped deep indoors,
Brown skin feeding his world's dark debauchery.

Nights yearned for nostalgia's tender embrace,
Yet home lay wasted, trust's fall from beauty,
Buried between images untrue I bore,
Lost in the painted illusions love constrained.

Unable to find myself nor home's arrival,
In the void my essence seemed to churn,
But know this, beneath the world's cruel roof,
Your identity thrives, your heart is home - Africa.

Bio: John Chinaka Onyeche is a multi-talented individual, wearing the hats of an author, poet, and educator specializing in History and African History. He boasts an impressive literary repertoire that includes works such as "Echoes Across The Atlantic," "A Night Tale At The Threshold Of Howl," "We Returned To Kiss The Cross," "The Broken Fort," "A Good Day For Tomorrow's Coming," "Stateless," "25 Atonements," and "The Gathering Of Reeds," scheduled for publication in March 2024 by Ethel Zine Press. Additionally, he has crafted a chapbook titled "Chapters Of Broken Tales." John's literary prowess has earned him recognition as a Best of Net Nominee.

FORGOTTEN

by LaVern Spencer McCarthy

I thought I was a memory,
a jewel my friends could own,
a glimmer in their velvet minds
now that my life is gone.

I thought they'd always think of me
that I might dwell among
them daily in a spirit's way,
my name on every tongue.

But all they do is rattle on
about the things they've done
and how the grass upon the hill
grows yellow in the sun.

Bio: LaVern Spencer McCarthy has published twelve books of short stories and poetry. Her stories have appeared in *Fenechty's, Anthology of Short Stories, The Writers and Readers Magazine. California Poppy Times Newspaper* and many others. She is a life member of Poetry Society of Texas and lives in Blair, Oklahoma.

IN ORDER TO ABANDON MY LITTLE TOWN,

by Claudia Santos

I cried
and fought
and studied hard.

In order to leave,
I left.

And I learned another language
so I could get a better job
so I could move to a different country
so I could only think of my own...

but I became an interpreter.

Interpreters never leave;
they never abandon;
we're trapped.

Your voice is his voice.
Her words are just your words.
These broken improper incomprehensible-to-anyone-but-a-native words,
these are my words.

These broken improper incomprehensible-for-anyone-but-an-in-between,
these are my words.

Bio: Claudia Santos (@claudiaexcaret) is a Mexican English Major, poet, interpreter, translator, and cultural gestor. She has been published in the digital magazine *Fleas on the Dog*, the printed anthology *Boundless 2022*, the Spanish magazines *Punto de partida*, *Blog Libropolis*, *Letralia*, *La poesía Alcanza*, etc. She focuses on promoting literature through her podcast Libros y otras cosas fuera del transporte and her youtube channel *La secta de los libros*.

REPARATIONS

by Terry Jude Miller

the lives of Blue Sky People
women and children
cannot be given back

they are given a mountain
their murderer's name erased
from its stone

drums and dancing
and ghost voices
call out from their heaven

should not their breath
be returned instead

Bio: Terry Jude Miller is a Pushcart Prize-nominated poet from Houston. He received the 2018 Catherine Case Lubbe Manuscript Prize for his book, *The Drawn Cat's Dream*. His work has been published in the *Southern Poetry Anthology*, *The Lily Poetry Review*, *The Comstock Review*, and *The Oakland Review* and in scores of other publications. He serves as 1st Vice Chancellor for the National Federation of State Poetry Societies.

CON AROMA DE CAFÉ

por Luis Alfonso Pérez Puerta

A través de ironías,
chistes forzados y malogrados,
nos enfrentamos a la existencia,
esa arma de doble filo,
y tratamos de cruzar al otro lado,
caminando por una cuerda floja
que lastima este cuerpo caduco.

Nos sumergimos en libros,
bailamos, gritamos,
buscando aliviar el peso aplastante
con un humor agridulce y,
en resumen,
así es como vivimos la vida.

Vivir con un toque de optimismo
no es sencillo,
pero "La Fuerza nos acompaña"
mientras saboreamos una taza de café,
quizá un poco de pan con mermelada;
o quién sabe, tal vez,
la bebida de los dioses.

Reseña: Comunicador Social - periodista, actor y escritor. Diciembre 1 de 1961. 62 años. Participo de los talleres literarios de escritura y el club de lectura que se llevan a cabo en las Biblioteca Comfenalco de La Playa, y en el Parque Biblioteca de Belém, el barrio donde vivo. Los libros han sido, y son, mis amigos, mis amantes, mis novios y novias; mi esposa, y mi vida. (Medellín, Antioquia, Colombia)

BULRUSHES

by Mahvash K. Mohtadullah

The bulrushes are whispering
Of secret things to come
I hear their murmurs when I pause
In life's frenzied thrum

Their words are indecipherable
Like runes on ancient walls
I know that I will understand
After their prophecy befalls

Still, I try this once to see
Through the hazy veil of time
To prepare myself in ways that are
Ephemeral, sublime

Everything happens when it must
Not sooner nor delayed
The murmurs become clearer as
We journey on, the sages say

But I try to circumvent
What nature has prescribed:
A time and place for everything
A cosmic order to all life

My mind rebels as I reach out
To visions beyond the glass
Willing a rip in space and time
To see things not yet come to pass

But the bulrushes keep whispering
Their murmurs wafting on the breeze
I know that when I'm ready
Then their secrets they'll release.

Bio: Mahvash worked in the Financial Services Industry. When she's not writing, she's fussing in her head over ideologies of social justice with superhero twists. Her stories and poems have appeared in *The Rumen*, *Sequoia Speaks*, *Recesses* and *Double Speak* magazines. Her poem, "Veins" was long-listed in the *Plough 2023* poetry competition.

ANGST

by Dr. Kanwalpreet Baidwan

The angst of dreams,
That lie scattered, crushed and trampled,
The angst of hopes broken,
Like shards of glass hammered and smashed,
The angst of being humiliated,
The self-respect and dignity mutilated,
The angst of wiping away one's smile,
And disabling one's laughter,
The angst of hiding that pain,
The sheer devastation of feeling wasted,
The angst of being a woman,
In a society that restrains and censors,
Smothers, stifles and subdues,
The conservative society,
Steeped in being morally right,
At the high cost of a woman's happiness,
Both mental and physical,
The angst of rising again,
Emboldened, energised and enlightened,
The angst of groping for identity,
And setting forth on a journey,
Despite the brickbats and all that jeering,
Behold the rise of the new Indian woman!
Who is not ready to indulge in self-pity,
The pleasure of having the will,
And the power of knowledge,
To chart out,
A future bright and beautiful,

With gritty teeth and a plucky courage,
Behold the Indian woman's excitement!
To turn the angst of merely surviving into,
An existence full of aplomb, bliss and control.

Bio: Dr. Kanwalpreet teaches Political Science at D.A.V. College, Sector-10 D, Chandigarh. She has written more than 100 book reviews for *The Tribune*. She has contributed articles for the *Times of India* and the *Hindustan Times*. She has presented papers in national and international conferences. She has presented papers at George Masons University in U.S.A and at the Bangladesh Liberation War Museum. She is a political analyst and is associated with many channels like BBC, CNN, Zee TV, India Ahead, Samvaad etc. Her poems have been accepted in *Syncopation, Yorick Radio, University of Wisconsin, Double Speak, Mocking Owl Roost, Open Skies, Fevers of the Mind, Borderless Journals* among others.

ENIGMA

por Diosa Xochiquetzalcóatl

(Poema inspirado por la pintura "Inmigrantes"
de Magdalena Martínez Mateos)

Sombras nada más.

Ambulando
lejos
de
sus
hogares

Sombras nada más.

Raíces
desterradas
regadas
por
el
mundo

Sombras nada más.

En
busca
de
mejores
vidas

Sombras nada más.

Penumbras
que
van
penando
siempre
añorando
el regreso
a la luz

Reseña: Diosa Xochiquetzalcóatl is a multilingual & multidimensional, slam/spoken word champion and international poetiza. Diosa X has been published in a variety of anthologies and literary magazines in the US and Mexico, and has published four collections of poetry. You can find more information about her and her work at https://linktr.ee/DiosaX

SPEAK TO THE HEART

by Barbara Anna Gaiardoni

But Mummy will go to heaven, won't she? The answer's no. I'm sorry. On the contrary, many caregivers would say yes. That lie helped them take control of children.

Death is a farewell. Death is not a place. Kids need time to take a moment to say goodbye. To adapt to a new existence made up of awareness. To give time to time. To build together a family memory, to discern the signs of freedom.

like worm's
metamorphosis
their soul

Bio: Barbara Anna Gaiardoni is winner of the First Prize 2023 "Zheng Nian Cup". Her Japanese-style poems have been published in *The Mainichi*, *Asahi Haikuist Network*, *Akita International Haiku Network*, *The Haiku Foundation*, *The Japan Society UK* and in one hundred and eighteen other international journals.

LIGHTS GO DIM

by Robin DeRosa

Love is not linear
Love follows the jabbing points
Going up and down like a heart monitor reading
Love is a choice

Often times hard to make
Love is a FUCK; why did you go?
Love is a FUCK; why did you stay?
Love is a rapid beat
Love is a faint thump
Love is spread to many
Love is given to none
Hurt me
Love is whatever you want it to be
Love is what drives me
I love you, and you, and you and him
Monitor Spike

Raging beep

Spikes drop
Then heighten
Repeat
I love you, and you, and you, and him
Love is a blind walk into an already dim
Room of sorrow and terrifying beauty
Dance with the shadows

Dance to the beat
Heart monitors beeping
I love you, and you, and you and him
A constant sweeping off our feet
I love you and you and you and him
Black me out

Lights go dim

Bio: Robin DeRosa, founder of The Nest Autism Support & Coaching, is a passionate advocate for the autism community. Diagnosed at 29, she leverages her experiences to assist autistic individuals and their families. Originally from the Mexico-Texas borderlands, Robin relocated to New Jersey in Feb 2024, bringing a blend of cultural richness to her new home. In her free moments, she expresses herself through poetry and photography, capturing life's complexities and beauties.

LEAVES

by Sunayna Pal

                like small flies
            abundantly found
through summer

red and yellows
            caught in the crosswinds
                    reverberate around me

                        before they end
            their dance to rest
in the ground

Bio: Sunayna Pal was born and raised in Mumbai, India, and currently resides in Maryland with her family. Her debut poetry book, *Refugees in Their Own Country* (B&W Fountain), explores the Partition of India. Her poetry is widely published all over the world and she is the Director of The Poetry Academy. Visit sunaynapal.com.

A DIOS

por Javier Villarreal

¿Cuánto tiempo hace de tu adiós?
Se repliega el pensamiento a la memoria.
Se entorpece el paso de los días.
Agobiado por este silencio atroz,
me pregunto:
¿Qué estará pensando Dios?

Reseña: Javier Villarreal, a Professor Emeritus of Spanish, holds a BA and MA in Spanish from Pan American University, Edinburg (UTRGV), and a Ph.D. in Hispanic Linguistics from the University of Texas at Austin. His works have appeared in numerous academic and literary journals and anthologies. His first poetry collection *Entre Lluvia, canto y flor* was published in 2008, and *Perfiles del silencio* in 2021. He edited *La voz de amor* of Servando Cárdenas in 2016. He is a member of the People's Poetry Festival. Javier retired from Texas A&M University-Corpus Christi in 2015. He resides in Corpus Christi with his family, where he writes, practices photography, and promotes cultural events in South Texas.

LAUNCHPAD MCQUACK

by Arturo Cortez Jr

No More *He-Man and the Masters of the Universe*.
And, perhaps, never again *Rocky and Bullwinkle-*

I'll listen to *Over-Nite Sensation* by Frank Zappa,
While I finish reading *Catch-22*.
I will also watch *Rashomon*,
Raging Bull, for the second time,
Rewatch *Taxi Driver*,
Tizoc and *La Vida No Vale Nada*,
The Battle of Algiers,
And I will add *The Sopranos*,
And *Amores Perros* as well.

No more Saturday-morning cartoons or cereal for me.

And maybe, moderate use of Prozac.

Bio: Arturo Cortez Jr was born in the Rio Grande Valley. He lived in Rio Bravo, Tamaulipas the first 14 years of his life. A major constant in his life has been creative writing. Donald Rawley (RIP) was the writer that ignited Arturo's spark as a creative writer.

US

by Fariel Shafee

We are made of layers of
Wants. Shards of emotions
Swirl around our gluey
Skin -- some sticking to us
For years, others falling off
When we move on.

How I loved you once,
Thought I'd never
be myself
If you deserted me.
Now I see you shout, curse and
leave, and I
Feel nothing.

Bio: Fariel Shafee was born in Bangladesh. She did her studies in the East Coast of the USA. Her experience with various cultures has made her think about the commonality of life. Besides writing poetry and prose, she also paints. Her writing credits and art can be seen here: http://fshafee.wixsite.com/farielsart

EL CAMINO SIN DESTINO

por Laura Peña

Camino sin saber el destino
las vueltas que da la vida
nos llevan a las cúspides

o a las tumbas
en que nos parecemos
en el deseo de caminar

sobre el sol
aunque nos quememos
terminarán en llamas

nuestros pensamientos
y valdrá la pena
encontrarnos tu y yo

en ese camino
sin saber
el destino

Reseña: Laura Peña was born and raised in Houston, Texas. She holds a BA in English Literature and an MA in Education. She has been published both in print and on-line. She was the featured poet at the April 2018 Valley International Poetry Festival. Laura received the Lucille Johnson Clark Memorial Award at the 2018 Houston Poetry Fest. Laura has been a featured poet at Inprint's First Friday and Public Poetry. As part of Invisible Lines she performed at "Welcome to the American Freakshow" and "Each New Journey; Actual Slices of the Fabulous Billie Duncan".

SWEET BABY

by Luisa Kay Reyes

While down on our luck once again
We stayed at a cheap weekly inn.
Filled with rough "construction" type men
We tried to stay safe in our den.

Yet, we had to step out to wash clothes
Since the laundry was down a few roads.
When out of the blue there appeared
A feline whose ear had been sheared.

With big wide eyes that were filled with delight
He'd follow me whether day or night.
And patiently wait for me outside
While guarding me with furry pride.

He never begged me for a treat
And basked in the sunshine on his street.
But somehow he would always know
When down to wash our clothes, I'd go.

He kept his distance every time
Small but healthy and in his prime.
Thinking of it as his duty
To protect me and guard me fully.

He was terrified of plastic bags
Having been beaten by low-life scags.
For him some thick and heavy work boots
Carried only frightening attributes.

He was tortured as a kitten
Yet by his goodness we were smitten.
He had cause to, but bore no ill will
So sweetly our hearts he fulfilled.

For his instinct was to run and hide
To take things safely and in stride.
But in time he learned his new name
And with love Sweet Baby became tame.

Bio: Luisa Kay Reyes has had pieces featured in "The Raven Chronicles", "The Windmill", "The Foliate Oak", "The Eastern Iowa Review", and other literary magazines. Her essay, "Thank You", is the winner of the April 2017 memoir contest of "The Dead Mule School Of Southern Literature". And her Christmas poem was a first place winner in the 16th Annual Stark County District Library Poetry Contest. Additionally, her essay "My Border Crossing" received a Pushcart Prize nomination from the Port Yonder Press. And two of her essays have been nominated for the "Best of the Net" anthology. With one of her essays recently being featured on "The Dirty Spoon" radio hour.

ANGELS

by Doug Croft

Did the angels cry
As they rushed to the scene
To enfold the children's souls?

Leaving bodily shells,
Destroyed on floors,
Crumpled over desks,
Huddled in corners,
Backs to walls.

Did angels carry those souls gently
Contrast to abrupt violence moments before?

Did ancestral hearts wail
With rage-filled anguish
Screaming "no," "not yet," "too soon"?

Shattered by immediacy of tragedy
Are children scared of the most brilliance of light?
Or feel the encompassing comfort of love,
Floating with swiftness upon angels' wings?

After the tragedy of violence,
Darkness of shock,
Enlightenment of evil,
Can precious little ones comprehend peace in forgiveness?

Bio: Doug Croft is a fundraising director. He has multiple anthology and journal credits. His first full-length poetry collection, *Exposed Roots*, was published in 2023. Croft resides in Charlotte, NC from where he travels to work on projects, and to see as many of his favorite rock 'n' roll bands as possible.

A SKY

by David Dephy

A sky grew within my heart, one day,
I was standing in the front yard.
A sky was so high it penetrated me through.
Oh, what a sky it was, so familiar and powerful
the memories as the leaves fell off the trees.
They were on the ground, as the imprints of glances
once when we saw each other for the very first time.

Bio: David Dephy (he/him) (pronounced as "DAY-vid DE-fee"), is an American award-winning poet and novelist. The founder of Poetry Orchestra, a 2023 Pushcart Prize nominee for Brownstone Poets, an author of full-length poetry collection *Eastern Star* (Adelaide Books, NYC, 2020), and *A Double Meaning*, also a full-length poetry collection with co-author Joshua Corwin, (Adelaide Books, NYC, 2022). His poem, "A Senses of Purpose," is going to the moon in 2024 by The Lunar Codex, NASA, SpaceX, and Brick Street Poetry. He is named as Literature Luminary by Bowery Poetry, Stellar Poet by Voices of Poetry, Incomparable Poet by Statorec, Brilliant Grace by Headline Poetry & Press and Extremely Unique Poetic Voice by Cultural Daily. He lives and works in New York City.

TRAIL LESSONS

by Charles Darnell

I walk this trail along
Leon Creek often enough
to feel at home,
every turn and hillock
familiar as the walkway
to my house.

The years of seasons
a cycle of life,
a slow rhythm of change.
The trees obey the rule
of life's circle,
budding leaves in Spring,
full splendor in Summer,
color palette each Autumn,
the dormancy of Winter.

I see my own life in slow mimicry,
now, in the late Autumn of my years.
My Fall color the deep tan of sun.

I know Winter comes,
the slow restriction of
movement, of mind.
I welcome it.

The cycle of renewal will follow,
not in my life,

but in life all around,
in the Spring leaves,
in the chirp of nestlings,
and the smile of grinning grandchildren.

Bio: Charles Darnell lives in San Antonio, Texas, and is a member of Maverick Poetry Group. His poetry has been published in many literary journals, magazines, and anthologies as well as the *San Antonio Express-News* and *Houston Chronicle*, most recently in *The Ocotillo Review*, *The Central Texas Writer's Society and Beyond*, *2023*, and the *2023 Texas Poetry Calendar*, His chapbook, *Water, Tongues, Earth and Blood* was published by Finishing Line Press in 2018 and his full volume of poetry, *Toward Human*, By Kallisto Gaia Press in 2022.

WHERE DO I STAND?

by D.L. Lang

I do not stand with you
when you bomb children.
I do not stand with you
when you shoot civilians.

I do not stand with you
when you take prisoners.
I do not stand with you
when you starve people.

I do not stand with you
when you elect fascists.
I do not stand with you
when you torture people.

Retaliation is not self defense.
Nationalism has blinded you.
I do not stand with flag waving,
warmongering, bloodthirsty bigots.

I mourn for the innocents.
If I must condone such horrors
in order to stand with you,
then perhaps, I never did.

Bio: Vallejo Poet Laureate Emerita D.L. Lang is an internationally published poet and spoken word performer. She received proclamations from the California State Senate, California Arts Council, and Vallejo City Council for her service as poet laureate. She is a member of the Revolutionary Poets Brigade. Visit dianalangpoetry.com

THE BUTTERFLY AND THE OLD WOMAN

by Dr. Santosh Bakaya

Ah, it was such a flamboyant butterfly.
Its wings shimmered in the early morning sun,
as it   went round and round in circles, a tad vain of its richness.
The old woman sitting in the patio of her old cottage
which stood amidst a blossoming meadow, throbbing with roses,
watched   riveted, tightening the rag- tag shawl around herself, and sighed.
The roses bobbed up and down, trying to impress the butterfly.
She looked at the mountains in the distance and at the butterfly
which now perched on a lonely strand of grass.
Lo! The strand of grass suddenly seemed to come to life.

Her eyes caught some bushes fringing a little stream,
towards which the butterfly was sailing.
Hovering over the bushes, it traced back its trajectory
swooping down on a bottle of pickle,
tickling the old lady into remembrance.
The bottle soaking the sun in her patch of lawn
glimmered, and was reborn- with tints of gold.

The old woman thanked the butterfly,
for, she knew not what, thoughtfully heading towards the lawn,
remembering the time long back,
when she was a pig- tailed girl chasing gaudy butterflies.
Her shuddering sighs merged
with the early morning breeze, and were lost

Bio: Dr. Santosh Bakaya is an internationally acclaimed poet, writer, essayist, editor, and creative writing mentor with more than twenty-four books published across different genres. Her TEDx talk on *The Myth of Writer's Block* is very popular in creative writing circles

THE LOST HERB

by Margaret R. Sáraco

At the base of the driveway, a small broadleaf plantain pokes
through sand, dirt, and concrete, cars roll over it, dogs sniff and trample,

people walk and joggers run past, blind to this nomadic plant,
far from other plants and trees able to wildly venture,

like the dandelion, its weedy, wonderful cousin
confused by some with the banana-like

Caribbean plantain, it bears no fruit, but edible leaves grow
in rosettes on its four-inch poor man's fiddlehead shoots

pan fried in oil, tastes like asparagus, separating seeds
from stem with teeth. European settlers brought

smallpox on their bodies and plantain seeds
on their muddy bottom shoes. Now and then, the

white-man's footprint, invading wherever they go.
And yet, Plantago major, sacred herb, humble herb, cure all,

a band aid, remedy for snake bites, poison ivy and tissue restoration,
the lost herb. One tribal nation calls it life medicine,

ancient knowledge stored in its leaves,
stubbornly existing,

while homeowners advised to control,
cut, weed, and saturate with herbicides.

Bio: Margaret R. Sáraco's writing appears in anthologies and journals, including *Boundless 2022*, She has been nominated for a Pushcart. Her books *If There is No Wind* (2022) and *Even the Dog Was Quiet* (2023) are published with Human Error. She is a poetry editor for the *Platform Review*. https://margaretsaraco.com

ESSENCE
by Dr. Tejaswini Patil

I remembered,
an old woman in a poem,
Scratching off her skin with a stone
On the bank of a river
To wipe out the eyes of men
That pierced her body
Throughout her life...

I thanked the cotton clothing
On my body saving the essence
Of a woman in me in the crowds.

And I learnt about my sisters
Being stripped off by the wild, uncivilised
Hands of men ...
They touched me, my body
There, thousands of kilometers away,
I shivered to bones.
They touched their bodies,
Patted their breasts,
Pierced through her vaginas,
Raped in front of the like-minded eyes, hands, and hearts,
And so on and on.... till their bodies sickened....

The two souls crushed and crushed
Putting all WOMEN in the world to shame...
(And they said, it was not the only case...)

Are they the same to provide their womb
To nurture those wild, insane masses of flesh ... ?

Bio: Dr. Tejaswini Patil Academician; Trilingual poet writing in Marathi, Hindi and English; Editor. Short-story writer; Founder Director, *Innsaei Journal* and *MatruAkshar Journal.* Three Collections of English and one Hindi poetry have been published. Recipient of National and International Awards for Non-Violence, Peace Pax Ambassador and Delegate, Argentina.

NIGHTLY NEWS

by John Grey

The TV informs me they're out there:
car-bombs, serial killers,
dictators butchering their own to stay in power.
And then there's the epidemics,
mosquitoes, ticks and fleas,
tiny living resentments
getting their own back at people.
And worse than that, the pandemic, Covid 19.
What did we ever do to bats?

Next up, the camera turns its ghoulish eye
toward my own neighborhood.
Drive-by shooting claims ten-year-old.
Child burnt in house fire,
found clutching the charred remains of a teddy bear.
A deadly three-car pile up.
A drowning in a pond.

Then there's the sports.
Such a relief
even though my team didn't win.
These losers traipse off the field,
but to the showers,
not the firing squad.

Bio: John Grey is an Australian poet, US resident, recently published in *New World Writing*, *California Quarterly* and *Lost Pilots*. Latest books, "Between Two Fires", "Covert" and "Memory Outside The Head" are available through Amazon. Work upcoming in the *Seventh Quarry*, *La Presa* and *Doubly Mad*.

FROM SANCTUARY

by Kendra Preston Leonard

I measured the earth and they
measured the earth and we came up with
different
different
differences
displaces

the architecture
falls

a sword on the neck
and no sugar anywhere

measuring a new earth and they
make the earth fit
the measurements I make

water all the time and
a model collective

difference
different
displace

no sword but so much sugar
in interviews and
diagnoses

small bowls full

trembling
ends

who owns what I used to own?
how do they measure it?

Bio: Kendra Preston Leonard writes about music, movies, gorgons, werewolves, Shakespeare, feminism, nature, ghosts, disability, drama, race, paleontologists, and much more.

DIASPORA

by William David

when not preoccupied with
the world i drew pictures of
battleships as a child

i was a navy commander
during autumn and winter

during spring and summer
an army ranger

why daydreams go unfulfilled
i believe must be the soul retreating

in a department store like a child
seeking its mother's attention
after venturing too far

like a diver with only air enough
to explore surface depths not able
to reach more wondrous deeps

Bio: William David is a resident of Edinburg, Tx. He works in healthcare and holds degrees in English and History. His work appears in *Odes and Elegies*, *The Windward*, and *Riversedge*, as well as *Boundless 2023*.

MAKERS, MOTHERS, OR CAPTORS

by Alex Carrigan

After Bethany Jarmul's "The Home I Abandoned"

The Appalachians as makers, mothers, or captors.
I had to learn my mountain was all three when I was young.

  When I was young, I clung to my mountain side,
  asking her to give me water and honeysuckles for nourishment.

Nourishment gave way to the dirtying of my hands when I realized
I'd have to find them myself, for the mountain asked me to search for them.

  To search for them along her sprawling limbs, I learned she was maker
  when I realized she left me runoffs and trails to find my continued survival.

My continued survival was dependent on how the seasons treated her,
how much of her remained with each passing year, what hadn't eroded away.

  What hadn't eroded away soon left me with no path down the mountain,
  for she wouldn't let me leave to share news of her bounty to my sisters.

My sisters cried when they realized I went up the mountain, for they also knew
that the Appalachians were makers, mothers, and captors.

Bio: Alex Carrigan (he/him) is a Pushcart-nominated editor, poet, and critic from Alexandria, Virginia. He is the author of *Now Let's Get Brunch: A Collection of RuPaul's Drag Race Twitter Poetry* (Querencia Press, 2023) and *May All Our Pain Be Champagne: A Collection of Real Housewives Twitter Poetry* (Alien Buddha Press, 2022).

THANK YOU

by Tom Murphy

Sitting on a polished granite slab
at your feet, Muhammad Ali.

A gorgeous yellow and black butterfly
a swallowtail dances about, no bee to be seen

As close as one ever gets to you,
Muhammad, in this lifetime.

My favorite quote of yours "Looking at life
from a different perspective makes you realize

that it's not the deer that is crossing the road,
rather it's the road that's crossing the forest."

Though I drive those forest crossings in search
of another moment it's hard knowing all

that I've known many cannot. Trying
to keep it real here, Muhammad Ali.

Your wasp arrived landing on the pavers.
Do not tread here if you're not ready to serve.

You're the man. You're the man, Muhammad
Ali. Fighting reality. Fighting for justice.

Fighting for love and peace.
Thank you, Muhammad Ali

Bio: Tom Murphy is a road poet who drives like a demon to spill his guts in your town. Murphy was the 2021-2022 Corpus Christi Poet Laureate. Murphy's books: *When I Wear Bob Kaufman's Eyes* (2022), *Snake Woman Moon* (2021), *Pearl* (2020), *American History* (2017), and co-edited *Stone Renga* (2017).

SUSTAINABLE

by Allison Whittenberg

eating eggshells
for calcium –
crushed to mush,
watered down
is this the future,
we pray for?
wanting not to waste
as waste fills our needs

Bio: Allison Whittenberg's novels are *Sweet Thang, Hollywood and Maine, Life is Fine, Tutored* (Random House 2006, 2008, 2009, and 2010). Her work has appeared in *Flying Island, Feminist Studies, Inconclast,* and *The Ekphrastic Review*. She is the author of the full-length short story collection, *Carnival of Reality* (Loyola University Press, 2022). Whittenberg is a six-time Pushcart Prize nominee.

SANTA ELENA CANYON

by Ann Howells

Spring lavishes sun across the Chihuahuan:
ocotillo bloom, lizards bask, agates glow,
while the lazy Rio Grande trickles
aqua and emerald.
Sheer rock walls soar skyward,
sunlight penetrates a narrow slit.
This canyon gobbles light
as a corn snake swallows a rat,
and I walk suspended in perpetual twilight,
deliciously cool, peer at the sky
as though through the wrong end
of a telescope.

Bio: Ann Howells edited *Illya's Honey* for eighteen years. Recent books: *So Long As We Speak Their Names* (Kelsay Books, 2019) and *Painting the Pinwheel Sky* (Assure Press, 2020). Chapbooks *Black Crow in Flight* and *Softly Beating Wings* were published through contests. Her work appears in small press and university journals.

MONET'S LILIES

by Anna Maria Mickiewicz

green leaves on a smooth surface,
they overgrow the canvas with pastels

in the depths -
strong rhizomes

vaguely outlined power
is hidden below reflections,
yet it curves planes
with war violet

London 2015-2023

Bio: Anna Maria Mickiewicz is a London-based poet, writer, editor, translator and publisher. Founder of Literary Waves Publishing UK. She writes in both Polish and English. Her works have been published in the United States, Great Britain, Australia, Canada, Poland, Mexico, Italy, Bulgaria, Hungary, El Salvador, Chile, Spain, and India. She was awarded the Gloria Artis Medal for Merit to Culture by the Ministry of Culture, the Cross of Freedom and Solidarity and the Literary Award. Joseph Conrad (USA).

RUTLAND 56

by Christian Garduno

I don't even know how we got here
now I understand how World Wars get started
you won't even look at me
and you know I *cannot* stand that
I ask you a stupid question
and you don't even bother to reply
that's the worst, that's the worst
you're just sitting there on the couch
looking at your phone
I'm at my desk
pretending to be writing about something else
then I throw out- Are you hungry?
again no reply
you have your back to me and I sigh out loud

I'm not going to cave this time
I'm always the one who caves
what in the world were we even fighting about?
I hate that I get so mad and shout incredibly cruel things
then you bring up something from the past
that has absolutely nothing with what we're talking about
and in the heat of the moment
I think of ending things like really ending things
and everything just goes red then when it winds down
I wanna take back everything I said
but I can't and I just want you to look at me
you're just sitting there on the couch
and I'm wondering to myself if maybe I should cave

Bio: Christian Garduno is the recipient of the 2019 national Willie Morris Award for Southern Poetry, a Finalist in the 2020-2021 Tennessee Williams Writing Contest, and a Finalist in the 2021 Julia Darling Poetry Prize. He lives along the South Texas coast with his wonderful wife Nahemie and young son Dylan.

AN HONORARIUM FOR SWOLLEN SOULS

by Okolo Chinua

Laugh into the darkness to become an echo for forced breaths...
Gaze at the sea as an umbrella opening parts,
For the affinity that draws one to suffering is a spark kindled at night,
When silence becomes bowls of soup forced down expectant throats.
Hope spins pitfulls of saliva in a cauldron mixed with tears.
The valley descent, a cry awakening heroes to seasoned plight,
There he sits, an honorarium for swollen souls...

Bio: Okolo Chinua is a writer who writes for many reasons, the beauty of tomorrow being the foremost. Currently, he lives and writes from the suburbs of Onitsha, Anambra State, Nigeria.

PAWNSHOP KID

by Dahlia Aguilar

pawnshop papi leads her in by the hand
indignity a door whose bell rings
entering or departing

pawnshop papi saves up
for anything he ever wanted
to sign it away and buy it back again

or lose it altogether saying
to hold us over and
don't tell your mother

pawnshop papi wins sometimes
wedding band and twelve-string

but loses mostly
turntable, jigsaw, six-string

for the long-haired white man behind the counter,
it's all the same

held on to it as long as i could, buddy
pawnshop kid leads
pawnshop papi with a tug on the elbow

as papi calls back
don't call me buddy
and the bell rings

Bio: Originally from Corpus Christi, Dahlia Aguilar is a consultant and writer in Washington DC where she resides with her son and two dogs. She has read at the American Poetry Museum and The Writer's Center, and was recently accepted to a writing residency Under the Volcano in Tepoztlan, Mexico.

COMPLIMENTARY MAP OF THE SUBCONSCIOUS

by Colin James

You smell the animals first.
Guinea Pigs or some such rodent
cages not cleaned for a long while,
edging towards invisible fences.
The yard is in need of a reorganization
ends at the road and risks
nominal recuperative repetitions.
Stairs lead up to a wraparound deck
splitting Ruskin's Pathetic Fallacy
right down the middle. Someone
stained the railings a red rust,
Uncle Malcom rolled his sleeves up
laid down newspaper kneeling, spent
his own money so chose the color.
Splotches of tactical anti moisture stabilizers
must be repeated every year.

Bio: Colin James has a couple of chapbooks of poetry published. *Dreams Of The Really Annoying* from Writing Knights Press and *A Thoroughness Not Deprived of Absurdity* from Piski's Porch Press and a book of poems, *Resisting Probability*, from Sagging Meniscus Press.

MUSIC MAKETH THE POETRY

by Trev Wainwright

January seems to be dragging, inspiration flagging
Let's hope in February things get clearer as my tour draws nearer
I've uploaded some more music to my usb in case my hire car has mp3
I can listen to what I chose,
Setting off to the theme tune from Hill Street Blues
Or driving across the plains things are going like a dream
From Dances With Wolves, The John Dunbar Theme
James Taylor singing Fire and Rain Luke Bryan and Play it again
Always a delight, John Denver singing "Don't close your eyes tonight"
My friend Clarke's variation on Pachelbel, as the drives going swell.
Or simply driving along listening to his beautiful Mario's Song
So many choices, from instrumentals to voices
And all the time it's giving me inspiration for my rhyme
But I couldn't end this ode
Without mentioning Rascal Flatts being led home by the broken road

Bio: Trev Wainwright still performing as Trev the Road Poet this will be his 14th time being published in *Boundless* his first in 2012, and but for covid has been a regular since then. Still one of the UK's most prolific travelling poets. He is often inspired by music while travelling.

ABUELA (DUPLEX)

by Christopher Louis Romaguera

Abuela is the definition of kindness
She would never eat the last piece of bread

Abuela's bread always lasts
Her stomach fails so she can no longer eat

Abuela secretly pours more vodka before you shake her drink
No matter what Abuela does, her hands always shake

Abuela cooks so the whole family can eat
Abuela says her stomach's too small to eat

Abuela won't let any harm come
Abuela eats pain, comfortably numb

Before the funeral, Abuela made you quiche to eat
Your friend is dead, so like Abuela, you can no longer eat

Abuela does everything to hold the family together
Abuelas hands shake as she holds the ashes of her brother

Abuela used to wait for the dictatorship to fall
The doctors don't know why Abuela always falls

Abuela's home was blocked by 90 miles, a the whole world
Abuela's heart bridged 91 miles for us to find a home

Abuela wont go back, there's nothing left for her there
Abuela can't go back, there's so little left of her here

Bio: Christopher Louis Romaguera is a Cuban-American writer who lives in New Orleans, Louisiana. He has an MFA in Creative Writing at the University of New Orleans. Romaguera has been published in *Passages North, Massachusetts Review, Latino Book Review* and other publications. He is a monthly columnist at *The Ploughshares Blog*.

SUMMER STYLE: FREE

by Connie Ramírez

The sun of a hot summer has beaten down on my face,
Hours lost with my friends, just another
Southside easy day. No commitments to
anything, so we can run free.
Cruisin' on our *bicis*, down several barrio streets,
Just poppin' yang, laughing & spilling tea.
Some days we chill at the park, before supper & before
the dark We go to watch our vecino boys, all pop yang in
their rivalries Shooting some hoops or playing baseball
on lush greenery. We ravaged all the soda pops & the
corner store snacks we bought: Chico sticks, Fun Dips &
cherry Blow Pops,
Hot Fries & Doritos, Mexsnax churritos &
some Donitas– Deliciously doused en limón
and some chile Valentina.
After a dinner to close the day, the humid evenings were made For
sitting on the stoop to hit "replay" on the boombox as it blares
& chimes Songs that hit the core & the echo of "summertime,
summertime". Mixed tapes and radio shows– all in tune
Repetition of groovin' breakbeats flow,
Synthesized keys and drum machines
Mixed with the vocals of Stevie B & Johnny O.
The crooning of heartaches & Gen X pangs,
Hypes of love give life to daydreams
Played out in a notebook of teenage fantasies.

Bio: Connie Ramírez is a writer and visual artist from the Chicagoland area. She currently resides in southern Texas. She has written several essays, poems, and short stories in both English and Spanish. Her work has been previously published by *The Acentos Review* and in Latinoliteratures.org.

TEXAS RANGERS

by Jonathan Fletcher

Like a rippling pool of water
above the brown horizon
of a Texas desert,
it's easy to see what I want:

Crisp, ironed dress shirts
and pants, polished,
spotless belts and boots,
cinco pesos for badges.
SIG Sauer P320s, too,
each clean as the hands
that unholster them.

Like the dry, barren border,
the truth is less forgiving:

Above innocent bodies
as dark as mine—each lassoed
around the waist, each atop
a pool of blood—several
Rangers pose on horseback.
A picture is taken.

Though no Sam Bass,
Bonnie and Clyde,
or John Wesley Hardin,
every kill is a source
of pride for them.

Even a cattle rustler or two.

Try as I might,
I can't help but unsee
the grainy,
black-and-white images.

I wish they were mirages.

Bio: Originally from San Antonio, Texas, Jonathan Fletcher, a queer, disabled writer of color, holds a Master of Fine Arts in Creative Writing in Poetry at Columbia University School of the Arts. His work has been published in *The Adroit Journal, Arts Alive San Antonio, FlowerSong Press,* and *The Thing Itself.*

PURO RIVERSIDE

by Ken Wheatcroft-Pardue

By the train tracks, two *borrachos*
are singing *narco-corridos*, off-key,
but with *mucho entusiasmo*. If I lived
in a gated-community, I'd miss out
on this culturally significant moment.
And the *quinceañera* dance rehearsals,
across the street in the front yard – awkward teen
boys with the girls always putting them in their places.
and the mariachi music piped into my backyard
on most every random Saturday evening.
And *el paletero* wheeling his cart
cooled with dry ice down the street,
the summer heat burning beneath him,
ringing his bells and *los niños con sonrisas grandisimas*
running, running, running.

Bio: Ken Wheatcroft-Pardue has had poems published in *The Texas Observer, Concho River Review, Borderlands, California Quarterly,* and two anthologies of Texas poetry.

AMONG THE RUSHES

by Trier Ward

Today her silken prayers have become lost in the
rough leather corset of misunderstanding,
cinched tightly against pinched flesh and held breath.
High heels make that ass look just right.
Shoes that hurt are the soul of beauty.
What are bare feet running through the night?
The skinned knees and splinters from strange trees,
the tangles? She shouts down at passing men,
"Come away, O human child!" Bound faery,
trapped essence smashed into a push-up bra
with lipstick on her teeth again, a lost
cracked cell phone by her hand as ants surround her legs.

Bio: Trier Ward is a mother, poet, and scientist. She lives in Albuquerque, NM. Her poetry has appeared in *The Nervous Breakdown*, *Bohemia*, *Chachalaca Review*, and *Mad Swirl*. She is the author of two collections of poetry: *Bruises and Love Bites* (Penhall Publishing, 2014) and the *Hollowscape* (Penhall Publishing, 2016).

ODE TO GLORIA WALKING HOME

by R. Joseph Rodríguez

Gloria walks the borderlands barefoot

    and soothes her body with ripened aloe vera.

        Lavender and eucalyptus scent her long walk.

            (Neither Cabeza de Vaca nor Thoreau are here.)

So many sisters wave across her homelands

    as she inches her way across the fields and lomas and valles,

        listening to the cantos of the chachalacas welcoming her home,

            sure enough she will meet los antepasados and her descendants.

Gloria stops at the schools she attended years ago.

Her name's still etched boldly on desks and in books and stories:

GLORIA EVANGELINA ANZALDÚA

        . . . carved deep in the spines and scribes' codices.

            Her name waves like a ribbon in the sky and on earth

                and flying flag-like across hemispheres and universes.

Gloria sits in deep meditation and reflection on the borderlands

as she turns pages and, like the tlacuilo, makes meaning of all that unfolds

in the worlds she inhabits and imagines for the people on a long walk home.

Gloria speaks languages that summon the people from their slumber

to act now in the present, to stand up taller and bravely in these times,

to make shields and armor and hope in the longest of hours and nights.

Gloria, sister, your name still sings in corridos and sonnets and stories

about wounds and scabs and scars in healing: some seen, some hidden.

Contigo, you whisper. *Caminando se siembra y con hermandad.*

Bio: R. Joseph Rodríguez writes poetry and prose in English and Spanish. He is a reader of diverse, multilingual, and borderlands literatures, including banned and challenged books. Joseph enjoys advancing the art of literacies in the lives of youth. He lives in Fredericksburg, Texas. Follow him on social media @escribescribe.

A PICTURE OF A TREE

by Chris Billings

It stands majestic
proud in an open field
branches stretched upward to the heavens
yet, for all its vivid colors
it is flat, motionless
lifeless
relying on a viewer
to breathe life into it
to imagine it to sway in a summer breeze
leaves rustling in applause
for the birdsong from an avian chorus
nestled within its branches
while squirrels scamper
up and down its aged trunk
scarred from decades of weather
worn from changes of the seasons
casting its reflection
on the surface of a nearby pond
inspiring poets and artists
to sing its praise

Without that imagining
it is simply a picture

it may be worth a thousand words
but it is not real, not alive
not providing shade for lovers
nor spreading seeds for new growth
it cannot offer food and shelter
to so many unseen creatures

it is just an image
of a passing moment in time
and if we're not careful
one day, not so far away
this just may be
the only way
to see that tree

Bio: Chris Billings is a member of The Maverick Poetry Group in San Antonio. He was a member of the former Sun Poets Society as well as co-host of their weekly open mics. In addition to self-publishing several books of poetry, his poems have also been included in various anthologies. He lives in Schertz, TX.

GUARIA MORADA

by Amanda Hayden

Spike focote, enflamed mombin, homespun heirlooms, heliconia growing wild in honeycomb hues, windchime words whispered through hooked novena necks into Chica calligraphy, mounds of firebird fruits, thick rinds sun-heated, protective layers, shadows like feathers, ruby spotted swallowtail, clay colored thrush, country girl, purple passion flower, easter resurrection radiance, glossy gumdrops suck the pear sugar sand, glisten silk sticky, thousands of orchid species with moonlit petals, edges of shapes, amorous succulent splendor, expectant spreading Saraswati smiles, blooming beebalm bellies, trumpet umbrella bushes, what is that word, the desire to taste something that is inedible? *Pica,* that's it, like the girl you once saw licking the bottom of her flip flop like a lollipop, like *tres leches* among banana gardens, pineapple guava, mint chocolate chip, cherry curve maraschinos, who can deny an orchid can look like a magenta-faced mantis, or an almond may yearn to be a pistachio unshelled?

Bio: Amanda Hayden is Poet Laureate and award-winning Humanities Professor. Featured in dozens of journals and anthologies, her debut collection, *American Saunter*, is forthcoming (FlowerSong Press, 2024), followed by her second, *Old World Wings* (Wild Ink Publishing, 2025). She lives with her family and rescue babies, including a special blind, three-legged pup.

GRAVITY AND THE HEART

by Stephen Douglas Wright

The heart vaults its chest
Dangles in black nothing
Gnaws at absence
Spits hot red life
Ventricles are drooping roots
Uncongealed weeping banyan leaves
Only the accidental spray
To happen to hit and nurse the thirsty earth
The strength of this heart's gravity
Pull the stars to earth

Tie the oceans and mountains with gift ribbon
Draw the moon into obliteration;
Hours gone and hours to come
Spiral too to its hollow center
But though the heart was mine
My tongue twists words into vines
I amble through thorn patches
Blood begets my exile
A basket raft of limbs bestrides
an emanating dip

Whose center is the circumference of centuries
I ride the rippling aftermath
The heart has superheated
Dangles me in an event horizon
Eats me whole
Spits me back to life

Bio: *Stephen Douglas Wright* is a writer and performer from the United States, living in Taiwan. His poems and stories have been published in previous editions of *Boundless,* and in other publications including *Menteur Magazine, Bengaluru Review, Harvard College Children's Stories,* and others. You can learn more about him at stephendouglaswright.com.

FIRST FROST

by A Hua

Some welcome sunset in a glass of wine.
Some use colors, brush and ink, painting the contours
of the land and mountain peaks.

October at the foot of Mount Wei, water whirls around the reeds,
silvery ice crystals settle and gleam.
On a Japanese maple winged seed pods perch, eager to fly.

Oh, how splendid! All the world's secrets
clear and bright.
Flowers mirrored in a raindrop. Heaven's blue dome in a grass seed.

— except the lotus pods in the pond, much wearier than before.

霜降

有人将落日斟满酒杯
有人用颜色笔墨, 勾画着
大地和山峰

十月的魏峰山下, 水绕芦花
银霜落下
一株鸡爪槭上站满了欲飞的翅果

多绚丽啊, 所有的秘密
都清晰明亮
水珠里有镜花, 草籽里有苍穹

—- 只有池塘里的莲蓬, 要比之前
苍老许多

Bios:

<u>About the poet</u>:

A Hua, born Wang Xiaohua, is from Weihai, Shandong province, northern China. Her poetry has appeared in such publications as *The People's Literature, Poetry Magazine, Mountain Flowers, Flying Apsaras and October* as well as in various anthologies. A Hua has also published several collections of poetry including *Cattails* (2016), and *What Makes My Heart Swell* (2021) through Shandong Publishing House. A Hua was an invited participant of Poetry Magazine's 25th Youth Poetry Conference. She is a student of the 31st Advanced Research Class of the Lu Xun Literary Institute and a contract writer for the Shandong Writers Association. While A Hua is an award-winning, widely published and much loved poet in China, she is almost unknown outside its borders.

<u>About the translators</u>:

Xuelan Su is a lifelong lover of poetry and student of the Chinese language. She read A Hua in virtual meetings with friends during the pandemic as a source of connection and inspiration. The depth, beauty and relevance of A Hua's poetry inspired Xuelan to share it, through translation, with the Chinese diaspora and English-speaking poetry world. Xuelan lives with her family in Seattle, Washington.

Ziying Fan is a 2019 Princeton University graduate. There she focused on 19th Century French literature, but also worked with classical and contemporary Chinese texts. In 2021 Ziying joined Xuelan as co-translator. In early 2024 she showcased this project as part of the Translating Minority Voices seminar series in Toulouse, France. Ziying currently works as a software engineer in Tokyo, but will begin a Masters in Comparative Literature in the fall.

Xuelan Su and Ziying Fan's translations have appeared in *LIT* magazine and *NOTIS Northwest Linguist*, and were short-listed in the 2023 Stephen Spender International Poetry Translation Contest.

FOUR CALAVERAS (1998)

by Avery C. Castillo

for Pilar

The table is set
& you,
will never be forgotten.

The cool air from the open window
flickers the flame of lit white candles,
an invitation to sit

on green chairs, empty and shadowed: for the rest-
less, the hungry, the lost, the loved, the found.

We hang your picture upon the mantel or somewhere
near, center your aromas that stick
and melt to lived wallpaper.

So, we feast together & remember
how you used to dance as gentle and hot
as a breeze seeping in from cracked windows

You,
are not forgotten.

The glow of the flame,
where black eye-sockets now
glaze your once laughing brown eyes.

I wish I knew the sound of your voice,
your secrets, your soothing touch

Now,
we are only caressed by new light
where we will meet, beyond
this mundane table set for two.

Bio: Avery C. Castillo is a Mexican American poet from Harlingen, Texas. She is an MFA candidate in Creative Writing at the University of Texas Rio Grande Valley. Her work primarily integrates Anzaldúan theory to honor life as a young Latina woman living with an invisible chronic illness since childhood.

I'LL BE THE FLOWER, YOU'LL BE MY BUTTERFLY

by Oke Flourish Oluwatimilehin

I'll be the flower, you'll be my butterfly
My beauty for yours- I'll watch you expeditiously grow
My juicy nectars will be your potency to fly
Nourishing you even as you dazzling glow

Through larvae till adulthood until eight
Till I see you flourish, bloom and charmingly sing
My petals supporting your every weight
Even as it kisses your tender wing

In the summer, while I wane and wither away
I'll helplessly watch you fly away and sway
But I'll forever cherish the moments we share
They're memories I'll cling unto even as I tear and wear

I hope other flowers treat you better
Cos you deserve the sweetest nectar
I hope you land on the softest petal
Not on destination as hard as metal.

Bio: Oke Flourish Oluwatimilehin is a young Nigerian writer with an exceptional writing prowess, she has won lots of awards and honors. She's a poet, a story writer, a content creator and a graphic designer. She writes in several genres including thriller, horror, science fiction, epic fantasy, and mystery.

ARAB WORLD

by Joselin Mejía Garcia

At the world's edge and of all civilization,
the sun rises from the east
and ends in the Middle East.

I was born in the year 2000 in Kabul,
between mosques and gardens,
a year before the unhappy valley of life.

At nine years old,
my ears heard the most heroic battle,
12 hours of bullets in Kamdesh.

I did not know of the arab spring,
nor from ISIS,
nor of the body of my decapitated brother.

Father, help us!
I saw the weight of the sky sink into my shoulders,
the same date: October 7 in Gaza and Afghanistan.

Be merciful of all
those who have been lost
at the time of death, on the iron sword.

I can keep my faith alive in the basement of a hospital
with my dead son
Wa Qur-rabbighfir warham
wa anta khairur-raahimeen.

The destruction
leads to a hard road,
My Lord, forgive and have mercy.

If you don't know the truth,
My name is Afghanistan, not Al Qaeda!
My name is Syria, not Al-Nusram!
My name is Palestine not Hamas!

Bio: Joselin Mejía Garcia. Her poems have been published in Mexico and Chile by the *UNAM, Bitácora de vuelos ediciones* and *La Gata Ediciones*. Her poetry has also appeared in the USA in the 2021, 2022 and 2023 editions of *The Anthology of the Rio Grande Valley International Poetry Festival*.

ADRIFT

by PW Covington

He scribed all his needs onto parchment
All his fears and dreams and fantasies
Sealed behind repurposed glass and cast upon the tide
Distillery green and corked

The years, for all their barnacles
And Sargasso grass and oil slicks,
Never expected, never overdue
Pregnant, dead, and living all the same

Sunbeat in the doldrums
Forgotten like that physicist's cat
Distillery green and ocean drifting, weathered

Currents carry poetry
And random notes
And artillery shells
And lovers' scrawl and letterings
Circumnavigating the core across the crust

Insulated in his own
Demand for self-identity
He never heard the laughing gulls above
Driven mad by the haunting tones of humpback whales, galactic
Distillery green and hoping for hurricanes and jagged reefs
Of some never-coming, ever-coming

Messiah
Lover
Audience

Bio: PW Covington writes in the Beat tradition of the North American highway. He is a past VIPF Featured Poet and a supporter of Indie expression in the RVG.

A multiple Pushcart and Best of the Net nominee, in 2019 his collection *North Beach and Other Stories* was named a Finalist in LGBTQ+ Fiction by the International Book Awards.

Covington lives just south of Historic Route 66, in Albuquerque, NM, where he has worked with film and television productions including *Better Call Saul* and *The Cleaning Lady*.

CITY OF ANGELS

by Maria Garcia

City of angels was where we met.

Made a bed
Stocked a kitchen
Played records
Made café
Smoked weed in Huntington Park
where the odd man
interrupted our peace

He was not the one
that made me flee the state

It was the leave(s)
the careless gesture
the return to first homes
the "I told you so's"

For a while, though,
angels in the city, we were.

Bio: Maria Garcia is a member of the human race, MFA student at UTRGV, a caregiver, and many more nouns and verbs.

THIS QUAKING EARTH

by Nathan Brown

~ for Mesut Hancer, and his daughter Irmak
Kahramanmaras, Turkey

The worst of the quake's aftershocks
shook your soul down to a deeper
level of the hell surrounding you.

All that was left for the eyes to see
were the pale fingers of a soft hand
on the dirty corner of her mattress.

Her blanket draped and drooping
to the rubble below... one giant
pink tear falling on broken tile.

A flag lowered after the battle.
      A loss in the war of all fathers.
           At least those who dared to love.

And whether this was a seismic
god, an angry earth—or some
act of geological indifference—

what does that matter to you now
and forever forward... as you sit
in the ruins of Kahramanmaras

with nothing left for a father to do
but stay put, lean forward in frozen
air, reach out... and hold the pale

fingers of that soft hand, as long
as it will take for them to come and
free the rest of what does not remain?

Bio: Nathan Brown is an author, musician, and award-winning poet living in Wimberley, Texas. He served as Poet Laureate of Oklahoma in 2013/14. He's published 26 books. His most recent collection of poems is *In the Days of Our Endurance*. An earlier book, *Two Tables Over*, won the Oklahoma Book Award.

CUETLAXOCHITL

by Sarai Garcia-Martinez

Sit with me as I make tamales
Cheater style
You see, I too have been gentrified
Or is the right word homogenized
Or better yet convenient-ized

Why make tamales when I could buy them
Other hands could make them
And I could just glutton

Why grind my own corn
Why raise my own pig
Why sit in the shadows of my ancestors

Sit with me as I make buñuelos
Cheater style
You see, I too am par baked
Trans fat removed
Pre-packaged and refrigerated

Why make buñuelos when I could buy them
Other hands could make them
And I could just sloth

You see Poinsettia, should I even call you that? Noche Buena
You see, it's not their fault that they don't know your birth name.

The lust for you caused botany greed and in
Cheater fashion you were commercialized
Plucked from your region
Mass produced for seasonal sensation

And here we are trying to explain
All wrath aside, that those are not your petals, they are your leaves that
turn color.
Your flower is the yellow buds in between.

Forgive my pride, I will correct people to call you *Cuetlaxochitl*
It's the least I can do, you see, I too have been anglicized.

Bio: Sarai Garcia-Martinez is thankfully over 40. She writes during the odd years. Happily married. Mother of 1 amazing boy. Advocate for native trees and a park design enthusiast. And on more than one occasion has drank too much coffee.

HARM'S WAY

by Antonia Salinas Murguia

There are no more ordinary days.

Danger has broken the comfort fence.
Trust has become meaningless,
for not even la policia can protect us.
Learning institutions that for generations
have provided knowledge
for society's continuance,
for a strong country,
has lost its stability.

There are no more ordinary days.

Shots heard from inside schools,
fear freezing our bodies,
panic taking breathes of our air,
blood spilling senselessly,
screaming never, never stopping,
and death is in our faces.

There are no more ordinary days.

Loss lives after precious lives,
mindless deaths by sick individuals
have broken our nation, our schools,
our promise of safety for our children.

Why?
How do we make it stop?
We must make it stop?
We can't take this anymore.
We are all in harm's way.

There are no more ordinary days.

Bio: Antonia Salinas Murguia is a retired teacher, poet, and artist. She is President of Alamo Area Poets of Texas. She likes taking poetry classes and has been published in different anthologies. She is currently a motivational speaker, and writing her poetry. She lives in San Antonio, TX with her family.

HOW TO WIN FRIENDS AND INFLUENCE MEN (IN UNIFORM TO ARREST YOU)

by Daniel García Ordaz

1. Have your period on the border wall.

2. Hang cloth feminine sanitary napkins to dry on the border wall.

3. Dress like a nun or La Virgen on the border wall.

4. Create "The border is the river. Duh." signs ala Alicia Silverstone in *Clueless* on the border wall.

5. Breastfeed your child on the border wall.

6. Kiss a hot girl on the border wall.

7. Graffiti "Isn't it ironic?" on the border wall.

8. Fake an orgasm on the border wall.

9. Register women to vote on the border wall.

10. Eat a phallic popsicle on the border wall.

11. Spray paint "Kilroy was her!" on the border wall.

12. Flash mob dance " . . . Baby One More Time!" on the border wall.

13. Hang lingerie to dry on the border wall.

14. Distribute free condoms for all the tax-payers getting screwed to pay for the border wall.

15. Don Make America Gay Again hats and have a patriotic rally on the border wall.

16. Invite all-female artists to sketch live female nudes on the border wall.

17. Perform a concert with "Pussy Riot" tribute bands on the border wall.

18. Read Gloria Anzaldúa's essays and poems on the border wall.

19. Carry posters reading "**FREE HAND**outs about **JOBS!**" on the border wall.

20. Take a friend "camping" on the border wall.

21. Dress like Barbie on the border wall.

22. Have boobs and a vagina on the border wall.

Bio: TEDx Speaker Daniel García Ordaz, a.k.a. The Poet Mariachi, is a teacher and serves as the 2023 McAllen Poet Laureate. His work has been taught and written about across the U.S. and abroad and he is a 2018 Pushcart Prize nominee. García has an MFA in Creative Writing from UTRGV.

I FLY WITH BLACK BIRDS

by Alejandro "Jando" Gonzales

I fly with black birds,
streaking across turquoise
skies, painted softly with
fuchsia cirrus clouds,
light as a whisper.
To the east, I observe
snow-capped *Sandias,*
cold violet stone,
emanating a serene
power, frozen in time.
Black-winged *Caballo Loco,*
my wild midnight stallion,
flows through twisting *rios,*
singletrack cottonwood forests,
defying gravity - we rise.
Gliding with four Canadian
geese, in v-shaped formation,
their brown feathers shimmer
gold in the evening sun,
guiding us to salvation.
In that moment, time ceases,
I am part eagle and part wind,
we are lightning connecting
Heaven and Earth.

Bio: Alejandro "Jando" Gonzales is a Software Engineer with a Master's in Deep Learning and Signal Processing. He's been published in "One Albuquerque, One Hundred Poets", an anthology of poetry in Albuquerque NM, and writes often about his experiences in the mountains and on the trails, forming connections with Earth and people.

FAMILY LIFE ON THE GATEWAY CITY

by Sylvia Elia Vargas Carbajal

Indeed, our gateway cities take deep.
challenges
When there's around so much walking adversity
since our land saw the saddened calamity
Of many immigrants with historical passages.

Our families have become resilient.
On the verge of death, the river
The news still causes us a little shiver.
For those lives remain productively persistent!

Our family lifestyle on the borderlands
Goes on too with beautiful moments.
enjoying gatherings with constant movements
With so much joy that cheerfully stands.

Both gateway cities share delicious drinks
when their adorable people cross back and forth
The bridge that is full of South to-North
And the customs agents barely blink!

On this border, most of our food is bicultural.
Our families can't live without certain meals.
Even the performing art in both cities appeals.
and everything seems transcultural.

Our family traditions are always uplifting.
because our routines project an impact
That is unforgettable as an outstanding act.
That entertains with an amazing show!

Los laredenses somos genuinely caring
as poems with forceful and thoughtful rhymes
Somos los eternos fronterizos that beat up the crimes.
Because we've remained spontaneous and always protecting!

Bio: Sylvia Elia Vargas Carbajal is a committed school leader and prolific poetry writer with an intense and enthusiastic personal involvement in academic and literary affairs since 1991. Her professional degrees include three Master's Degrees from TAMIU in 2013- Master of Science in Educational Administration, 2003 -Master of Arts in Spanish, and 2001- Master of Arts in Interdisciplinary Studies Spanish. She has been an educator for the past 32 years promoting her assistance in multiple school committees. In addition, she has been a writing collaborator at *Del Alma Publications*, *Apariciones, Voces, Ruidos, Cosas Inexplicables: An Anthology of Folktales & Personal Narratives from the Texas-Mexico Borderlands*; she has been a recurrent English and Spanish poetry writer at the *Dos Laredos Communities: Laredo Morning Times* and *El Mañana, TAMIU, La Carta,* and has been a poetry winner several times of multiple contests.

CLOSER TO HOPE

by Mark Esperanza

Every year my baby girl is there
In the corners of playgrounds
Behind elementary school doors
Learning how to grow
Teaching me algebra
She's there
In the shadows of her sister's bedroom
Playing with dolls and tickle fights
Crying because she didn't get her way
Smiling because I'd eventually give in

She'd be ten now
Eleven this month
Snow White and wavy black hair
Button nose and sunflower eyes
Her cheeks are smaller now
Baby fat lifting away
Revealing a child on the edge of teenhood
But not yet
Still my little girl

I see her in the front door
Running up and racing for a hug
She's there with her sister
And I've got one in each arm
I lift them both to my face
Push back their hair and kiss their foreheads
We smile at each other
The three of us
And everything is okay again

I see her all the time
And everywhere
She's getting closer now

Bio: Mark Esperanza is an Edcouch-Elsa writer and currently teaches in the US-Mexico borderland city of Mercedes, TX. He has been published in numerous anthologies such as *Lamar Press' Writing Texas* and *Boundless 2023: the official anthology of the Rio Grande Valley International Poetry Festival*. Esperanza will be working towards his principalship and is expected to graduate December 14, 2024.

WON'T WRITE

by Érika Elisa Garza Tamez

Quisiera quitarte de mi pensamiento
Intento inspirarme,
inventar nuevos versos
Soñar sin sentir,
sin crear cursis cuentos
Finalizar, finiquitar
de una vez por todas, no
Unir un destino con aguja e hilo, ni
Mandar mensajes
subliminales sin sentido,
Esperar escribir
por un tiempo indefinido ni
Tatuar con tinta indeleble
tu recuerdo, ni
Pintar promesas pasadas
de futuros fríos
Ya yo llegué al límite,
no escribiré más de ti

Bio: La profesora y poeta Érika Elisa Garza Tamez es méxico-americana. Tiene una maestría en Español de la Universidad de Texas- Pan American. Sus escritos han sido publicados en numerosas antologías, tales como *I SING: THE BODY*, *Flora Fiction*, y *Boundless 2019-2023*, entre otras. Es autora del poemario *Con alas de mariposa*.

HOME IN MEXICO IS

by Sandra Arenas Salazar

where the zaguán negro is
(that's black door in English),
a big house in the city
(but not in La Condesa, Polanco or La Roma; deep in Iztapalapa),
a gardened house.

not a Pueblo Mágico
(my feet have learned to walk)
not a yellow filter
(in the dark)
not a desert or a blue beach
(of this noisy polluted crowded city)
the city
(traveling through the labyrinth of metro Pantitlán).

a nuclear family
(with secrets)
isolated
(in a bubble)
no tías, no primos
(there aren't any)
barely two abuelas
(with different skins).

a language being invaded
(my tongue has divided
but I'm still)

home.

Bio: Sandra Arenas Salazar. Member of the research collective PoeticaSonoraMX since 2022, legal assistant, and songwriter. Currently working on her bachelor's dissertation for the degree in English Literature by UNAM. Her poems and short stories have been published in print and online publications such as the *RUME*, *Universo de Letras UNAM*, and *Ágora*.

A BLAZE AMONG SMOKE

by Victor M. Parlatto

Bella,
the genuine soul is rare.
and it often arrives when nothing
does. it sits beside us with
a genuine smile and complimenting eyes.
it comes already loved and ready to love.
it is a somber glow of joy that cannot be
harnessed or tampered with.

and one always feels good when they're around it.
it's an immediate overflow of restlessness
and uncompromised satisfaction.

even on terrible days,
even on days with nothing, no money, no love, no way;
it comes into a room,
smiling, wearing
a simple ankle bracelet,
and embraces you away from all the familiar shit.

sometimes it is all someone needs.
sometimes it is all anyone
wants.

but
the genuine soul
is as it is—

a blaze among
smoke;
a release from the setting migraines;
a sweet winter rose with blonde petals
ready to kiss the rain of midnight.

Bio: Victor M. Parlatto is a poet, father, and writer. With over a decade of experience, Victor has written countless poems and literary works. Well known for his poems addressed to Bella, Victor's poetry paints a picture of everyday life and the emotional spectrum in a comedic, dark, and occasionally brutally honest light. Victor attends poetry readings weekly and shares personal readings across his social media platforms alongside his written work. Some of these works include: "strip joint from the yellow pages" and "the greatest literary critic I have ever had". When Victor is not immersed in his writing, he spends his time with his daughter, gaming, reading, or listening to music.

MONTEVIDEO, CITY OF ROSES

by John C. Mannone

The harbor water curls sunlight
like a cup of roses

Surf's swish muffled by the rustle
of eucalyptus leaves in the park

and my sister is strolling
the baby carriage with me in it—

I'm barely two; she, only eleven
and my careful mother for now

She stumbles—ground shadowed
gnarled with roots—scrapes her knees,
                            bleeds

I search her face, listen for her crying
so I too can cry—

        I only hear the salt wind,
        the soft-tongue warblers

but I can see her heart
blossoming
            like a rose.

Bio: John C. Mannone has poems in *Windhover, North Dakota Quarterly, Poetry South, Baltimore Review,* and others. He was awarded a Jean Ritchie Fellowship (2017). His recent collection, *Song of the Mountains* (Middle Creek Publishing), was nominated for the Weatherford Award. He's a physicist teaching creative writing and mathematics in Tennessee.

THE CACTUS BLOOMED PURPLE FRUIT

by Linda Feliciana Romero

I hear the crunch of the brittle and yellow grass under my feet as I walk
out back of my aunt's house

I imagine how the land looked when my grandfather farmed okra,
farming mostly alone,
My family living in the house he and my Tio Antonio built

Mesquites, Anacuas and **Huisache dance in the humid breeze where the
house once stood,**
where my aunt built her house decades later
They shade around the property,
inaudibly crying and speaking what they have witnessed and endured,
they stand in testament to all those decades before me

I'm now looking for a succulent in the far corner of the property
A couple yellow butterflies flutter around me as my boots fall on the tall
blades waiting to be bailed
They keep me company as I take visual inventory of what has changed
since last week

The cactus I found on the end of the property bloomed purple fruit

Bio: Linda Feliciana Romero is from Harlingen, Texas and has been
published in *Boundless*, the anthology for the Rio Grande Valley
International Poetry Festival, *Along the River 2: More Voices from the
Rio Grande* (VAO Publishing), *Twenty: In Memoriam* (El Zarape Press),
and *La Bloga*. She was nominated for a Pushcart Prize in 2018 for her
poem, "In the Passenger Seat" by El Zarape Press which appeared in
Boundless 2017. She is a Certified Academic Language Therapist and
has a private practice providing dyslexia therapy.

WING LOVED DOVE

by Naomi Alegre

I often convince myself
I've forgotten what you did
            what I allowed, such shame you bring

The days at bars & clubs are long gone
Trying to find the love of my life off Cosmos & Pornstars

I can't remember to dance the way I used to
As you tossed me your final rejection

I've been a fool for love
Oh, I've known from the start
That this too would go down bad

But I ran & flew after you with wings
When all you were doing was trying to get away from my feathers
Faster than it took my bleeding heart to dry its crimson tears

I took one look at my wings, plucked my feathers one by one
I'd become bone
    become human like you

Didn't feel a furnace in me
I felt nothing but the blood I'd wasted on someone who didn't mind
crushing
Their wing loved dove and suffocating it as it took its last breath

A breath that meant it loved you more than anything
But it would never be you and when the dove arrived at heaven
It closed its eyes and tried again

Bio: Naomi Alegre is a Mexican American poet born and raised in Brownsville, Texas. Currently an undergraduate student at UTRGV, she is set to graduate Spring 2024 with a B.A. in English. Her poetry aims to help her emotionally connect with others.

CREATE THE WORLD, WE ALL WANT AND NEED

by Vito del Valle

Keep pounding on the tables
Keep marching in protest
Keep living truth to power
Make steel traps out of hearts and minds

Never settle on wages
Never walk the wrong path
Never snitch on your neighbor
Create words out of blood and bone

Always keep your head up
Always be proud to choose
Always raise your fists
Build a tomorrow without greed and poverty

Love every person
Love every tree
Love every animal
Forge a future with justice and humanity

Stand up to corruption
Stand against oppression
Stand next to your brothers
Create the world we all want and need.

Bio: Vito del Valle is a Chicano writer/musician from Donna, Texas. Vito's work has appeared in *Boundless Anthology 2022* & *2023*, *The 2023 Northwind Treasury*, *South Texas College - The Writer's Block*, and *Interstice*.

CONTEXT

by Jonathan Salinas

Tell me about the shapes, dimensions, spheres of influence That
surround, encapsulate, incubate, some might say Tell me about the
history, short and long, here and there Which may or may not reveal
while it itself is revealed Memory cannot be shared, in common, with or
without All memory is propaganda
Propaganda of the false self
Blurred, distorted, confected, confabulated
The present may not either be agreed upon
Eyes lie
Ears deceive
Lips betray
Don't believe the truth, they say
We think, therefore we might be
Strong enough, objective, lucid
In vain dwells unpleasant questions
Nevertheless, an escape can be found
In every word

Bio: Jonathan Salinas is an RGV native, writer and musician. He's
written for a number of publications as a staff writer and contributor
including the *Brownsville Herald*, *Neta (now Trucha) RGV*, and the *Rio
Grande Guardian*, as well as regional and national outlets. He currently
writes a weekly cultural, political column on *Substack.com*.

BEAM OF LIGHT

by Aldo Cristian Méndez Castillo

My heart feels the soft warm,
silent pleasure from your smile,
indeed you are the love of my life,
light of hope, a beautiful paradise.

Behind the window of my soul
a beam pierce through silence,
a dream coming to life, it is you,
muse and lover, sweet madness.

Beyond the sky memories come,
thousand lives lost in poetic love,
your light embraces both of us,
eternal sun, our fountain of youth.

In poetry I reach the stars,
each one, a wish to fulfill,
words in love, just as I am,
I write again, with you in my arms.

Bio: Aldo Cristian Méndez Castillo nació en Ciudad Valles, San Luis Potosí, México, el 06 de octubre de 1980. Su pasión principal es escribir poesía en español y en inglés. Ha logrado que algunos textos de su autoría sean publicados en plataformas digitales y antologías como "Boundless 2023"

BRING BACK MY FALL AND WINTER

by Mia Cervantes

Bring back my sweet darkness
my long nights and empty wine glasses
my cozy throw blankets with textures that ease my anxious thoughts
beautifully gloomy inclement weather that
makes it easy to come up with an excuse to
cancel plans I made with potential new friends

Bring back my winter wardrobe
my layers upon layers of scarves and cardigans that cover
vain attempts at finding emotional comfort at the bottom of party sized
potato chip bags
my freshly baked cookies and hot cocoa with
fluffy white marshmallows floating at the top
and my quiet acceptance of the way things are
desiring nothing more
desiring nothing less

Bring back my fall and winter

Go ahead and keep your desolate Summer and
take back your wretched scheming hostile Spring that brings
false promises of rebirth with every blooming blossom
lies of change in the nests and dens of new mothers
distracting hues of vivid colors that hold the truth of suffering
hostage among hosts of golden daffodils

I know the fragrance of fresh cut greenery in the air is only there
to mask the odor of decaying bodies of hope lying
within every smiling person I walk past

my mind will never again be prey to spring-time follies and
dreams that will never come to fruition
I vow my heart is now forever protected from blinding beams of sunshine that leak
cancerous ultra-violet rays into the core of my existence
I am no longer one of Springs foolish victims

Bring back my fall and winter

Bio: Mia Cervantes is a writer and artist from Los Angeles California currently living in the RGV. Mia began writing poetry to help her cope with trauma and feelings of being disconnected from the people around her. She aims to create pieces that remind others that they are not alone.

FLYING KITES IN THE WATER

by Demian Palacios

In the flight where wings are born
it gets late also when the sun rises,
with some eyes calm in the water,
We learn to swim by flying kites.

Sailors in dreams of wooden meadows
the pigeons' mornings are moving, disturbing and flying,
on the road where the trains gallop;
in these minutes when the time is getting old.

So, I share the the afternoon's delusions,
when everything wants to get dark,
in the south that mistreats us by sounding like yesterday,
like someone returning to carnations
and to the words when they are crossing the streets.

There are no more roses,
this time the fall took away the days
in between the rain and the dry leaves;
that are alone,
like the sunsets that used to be clear.

It's like the wind's half that becomes part of the smoke
that leaves and comes in water.
Sometimes by moving the heart from your chest
Against your sleep; counting evenings like stars

And in the winter we also become clouds
in these stars covered by light.

Bio: (Demian Palacios, Mexico) In 2018 he published his first book: *Donde se hiela la sal del mar* (Ediciones Del lirio). He was published in the *Naufrago Magazine* presented at the 7th International Book Fair of Arquetopia, Peru. His poems have been published by *UNAM*, *Verso Destierro*, *El Canto de la Alondra*.

ONCE, FOR A MOMENT, PEACE RESTED OUTSIDE MY WINDOW

by Julie Brandon

I heard its sweet song
When I approached, it fled
To the countryside, to the cities, to the warzones
To the tunnels, the bombed-out buildings
Never staying long
Always just out of reach
I long to see it again
Not to capture and keep in a golden cage
Peace not shared withers and fades away
A memory of what could have been
But to learn the melody so that others may sing along
When we do, peace will finally have a place to rest

Bio: Julie Brandon is a poet, playwright and lyricist. Her work has been published in *Bewildering Stories*, *Awakenings Review*, *Shemom*, *Poetica Magazine*, *Am Yisrael Chai Anthology*, and *Corner Bar Magazine*. She lives in a suburb of Chicago.

WORLD CHAMPIONSHIP BULL RIDER

by Susan Beall Summers

At the convenience store, he told my sister,
"Yore the prettiest thang I've seen since I've got to town.
Kin I follow you home?"
and he did.

I was twelve, drawn by the sound of laughter in the den,
I froze in the doorway when I saw him
Big black cowboy hat,
long, thick mustache,
western cut dress shirt,
huge silver and gold
championship belt buckle,
Wrangler jeans,
black boots.

He was too big for the room
and entertaining my sister and mother with a road story.
At the end of the tale, he looked full at me.
I braced myself against those penetrating eyes.
"And who's this little heifer?" he asked.

I didn't know what a heifer was.
I hoped it was something wonderful.
It sounded so exotic;
I was nearly in a swoon.
He sat down and told rodeo stories for hours.

Later that summer, much to my shock and dismay -
my sister turned down his marriage proposal

and discovered he had also asked one of the girls
whose daddy owned the ranch where he was staying
and working.

He did what cowboys do and moved on to the next rodeo,
other young heifers, and that elusive 8 second ride in the spotlight.

Bio: Susan Beall Summers (Palacios, TX) has traveled from South Georgia swamps to Egyptian Pyramids to Philippine Islands to discover she enjoys teaching chemistry, helping students compete in poetry and prose for UIL, and living beside Matagorda Bay with her dog, Ollie.

Publishing credits include *Ilya's Honey, Di-Verse-City, Boundless, Heroine Chic, Crab Fat, Cattails, Frog Pond, Silver Birch Press, Equinox,* and others.

NO MORE TEARS FOR AMERICA

by Meliton Hinojosa Jr.

I saw when John was shot in Texas
I saw and shed tear
I was a young man then, very young

I have no tears for America
I saw when Bobby was shot in California
I saw and I shed a tear
I was a young man then

I have no tears for America
I saw when Martin was shot
Standing on a balcony in Memphis
I was a young man, too young

I have no tears for America
I was there in Uvalde's school shooting
I saw children and teachers shot, some dead even children
I am much older now

I saw the mall shooting in Allen, Texas
Some people running, the ones that could
Children and adults dead
Yes I am an old man now

I saw a van run over immigrants in Brownsville, Texas en el Valle
Some immigrants lying on the pavement waiting for a bus
Young and old dead
I am an old man now, with no tears left

America, don't let the rhetoric
From the left shape you
All that liberal nonsense
The extreme left

America, don't let the rhetoric
From the right shape you
All that right conservatism

America, don't let the rhetoric
From the undesirables
Decide for you
The confused ones

America, don't let the rhetoric
From the politician's shape you
The liers and the thieves
They all speak with forked tongues

America, don't let the rhetoric
From the pulpit
Decide for you
Just follow Jesus

I don't need a thank you for your service
Not from a community that doesn't understand
Not from those that celebrate freedom
Freedom is not free

I don't need a thank you for your service
Not from church that only cares about saving souls
Not from a bunch of comrades that only gossip
Not from you or you, or you

I don't need a thank you for your service
Not from a president that did not serve
Don't need an empty, thank you
I thank my brothers and sisters that served next to me, thank you for
your service

|| **Bio:** Meliton Hinojosa Jr. Chicano poet. Period.

LA NOCHE ESTRELLADA

por Gabriel González Núñez

Poema ecfrástico a partir de la pintura homónima de Vincent Van Gogh

Van Gogh plasmó lo nocturno,
opacó el cielo diurno.

Vio unas estrellas ardientes,
captó faros relucientes.

Se estremeció ante la luna,
la hizo ardua como ninguna.

Sintió unos soplidos finos,
los convirtió en remolinos.

Trazó unos cerros azules,
recatados como tules.

Previó un pueblito soñado,
lo pintó como apagado.

Puso árboles como llamas,
coquetos cual par de damas.

Van Gogh de los girasoles,
hombre de los mil dolores…

Vincent que tanto lloraba,
gemía cuando pintaba…

Vincent, nunca sospechaste
el fulgor que nos legaste.

Reseña: Gabriel González Núñez es profesor de la Universidad de Texas en el Valle del Río Grande. Ha publicado once libros para niños (Penguin Uruguay 2019, 2020, 2021, 2022, 2023), el poemario *Ese golpe de luz* (FlowerSong Press 2020) y el plaquette digital bilingüe *El ciclo / The Cycle* (Center for Latter-day Saint Arts 2020). También es autor de la colección de cuentos *Rumbos* (Jade Publishing 2021). Además tradujo el poemario *Vaho / Mist* (de Javier Fuentes Vargas) y *Yo soy Romero* (de David A. Romero). González Núñez es oriundo de Montevideo, Uruguay.

For details, visit our website at
valleypoetryfest.org

www.ingramcontent.com/pod-product-compliance
Lightning Source LLC
Chambersburg PA
CBHW011222120626
46545CB00010B/3115